Encyclopedia Brown's Book of the Wacky

OUTDOORS

OTHER ENCYCLOPEDIA BROWN BOOKS
BY DONALD J. SOBOL

Encyclopedia Brown, Boy Detective
Encyclopedia Brown and the Case of the Secret Pitch
Encyclopedia Brown Finds the Clues
Encyclopedia Brown Gets His Man
Encyclopedia Brown Solves Them All
Encyclopedia Brown Keeps the Peace
Encyclopedia Brown Saves the Day
Encyclopedia Brown Tracks Them Down
Encyclopedia Brown Shows the Way
Encyclopedia Brown Takes the Case
Encyclopedia Brown Lends a Hand
Encyclopedia Brown and the Case of the Dead Eagles
Encyclopedia Brown and the Case of the Midnight Visitor
Encyclopedia Brown Carries On
Encyclopedia Brown Sets the Pace
Encyclopedia Brown Takes the Cake
Encyclopedia Brown and the Case of the Mysterious Handprints
Encyclopedia Brown's Record Book
of Weird and Wonderful Facts
Encyclopedia Brown's Second Record Book
of Weird and Wonderful Facts
Encyclopedia Brown's Third Record Book
of Weird and Wonderful Facts
Encyclopedia Brown's Book of Wacky Crimes
Encyclopedia Brown's Book of Wacky Spies
Encyclopedia Brown's Book of Wacky Sports
Encyclopedia Brown's Book of Wacky Animals
Encyclopedia Brown's Book of Wacky Cars

DONALD J. SOBOL

Encyclopedia Brown's Book of the Wacky OUTDOORS

Illustrated by Ted Enik

WILLIAM MORROW AND COMPANY, INC.
New York

AUTHOR'S NOTE

All the stories in this book are true, except for those in Chapter 7.

In compiling this book, I received generous help from the following outdoor writers: Perk Angwin, Charley Dickey, M. Timothy O'Keefe, Bob McNally, Don Mann, and Charles Waterman.

Most of all, I am indebted to Bill Hallstrom, conservationist, outdoorsman, writer, and friend.

—DONALD J. SOBOL

Library of Congress Cataloging-in-Publication Data

Sobol, Donald J., 1924–   Encyclopedia Brown's book of the wacky outdoors.
Summary: A collection of humorous anecdotes, most of which are true, about outdoor life, with an emphasis on fishing and hunting.
1. Hunting—Anecdotes, facetiae, satire, etc.—Juvenile literature. 2. Fishing—Anecdotes, facetiae, satire, etc.—Juvenile literature. 3. Outdoor life—Anecdotes, facetiae, satire, etc.—Juvenile literature. [1. Fishing—Wit and humor. 2. Hunting—Wit and humor.   3. Outdoor life—Wit and humor.]   I. Enik, Ted, ill.   II. Title.
SK33.S6455 1987   799'.0207   87-7851
ISBN 0-688-06635-6

To those outdoorsmen whose efforts in the cause of conservation have helped preserve what remains of wilderness America

Contents

The Case of
the Invisible Ray Gun

Encyclopedia and Sally Kimball, his junior partner, were sitting in the Brown Detective Agency when Harry Hilibrand entered.

Harry was nine and loved birds and animals of all kinds. He spent his summers tramping through woods and fields listening for wildlife sounds.

"Heard anything new lately?" Encyclopedia asked.

"Money talk," Harry answered. "Wilford Wiggins has called a meeting this afternoon at five o'clock in the city dump. He says he has a gun that helps feed starving young birds that have been abandoned. It shoots a silent, invisible ray."

"Oh, no." Encyclopedia groaned. "Doesn't Wilford ever quit trying?"

Wilford Wiggins was a high-school dropout and too

lazy to snore. He lay in bed till noon, planning ways to cheat the children of the neighborhood.

"Wilford promised to make us little kids so much money, we'll live like the idle rich," Harry said.

"When Wilford offers you a red-hot opportunity, be careful how you grab it," Encyclopedia warned.

"I know," Harry said. "So I stopped by to hire you." He laid twenty-five cents on the gas can beside Encyclopedia. "I want you to hear Wilford out and give me your advice."

Encyclopedia agreed. He had stopped Wilford's get-rich-quick schemes in the past.

A little before five o'clock, Encyclopedia and Sally biked to the city dump. They found Harry in the crowd of excited children.

"The meeting is ready to start," Harry said.

Wilford stood atop a rusty old elevator car, trying to look on the up-and-up. At his feet was a bird's nest.

"Gather 'round, friends, gather 'round," he called.

The children moved closer. They were eager to hear Wilford's latest money-making deal.

"Now, I'm not going to fast-talk you," Wilford began. "You all know me. I've always been straight with you."

"Straight as a rainbow," Encyclopedia muttered.

"Every year another species of bird dies out," Wilford declared. "Can anyone save the birds, you ask? Is there no hope?"

"Cut the sales talk and get on with it," Jody Turner shouted. "What are we waiting for, an early snow?"

Wilford grinned. "Ah, impatience. The sweet smell

2

of money! Makes the nose twitch and the tongue wag."

He pointed to the bird's nest at his feet.

"Inside the nest are three baby birds, so young that their eyes aren't opened yet," he said. "Their mother and daddy flew away and left them to starve! They won't die because I can feed them—with the help of this!"

He drew a small black gun from his pants pocket. He glanced around slyly.

"This gun will help feed the birds of the world!" he exclaimed. "Never again will scientists have to remove starving baby birds from their nests to feed them. The silent, invisible rays from this gun make the baby birds open their mouths wide so they can be fed properly. At home. In their nests!"

"Show us how it works," said a big blond boy. Encyclopedia had never seen him before.

"I'll show you, friend," Wilford replied. "Watch closely." He bent over and pointed the gun at the nest.

"Hold on," the big blond boy called. "If that's a silent, invisible ray gun, how will we know when you've fired it?"

"I'll touch the nest lightly with my other hand and fire the gun at the same time."

The crowd of children tensed. All eyes were on Wilford.

He squatted down. His left hand touched the rim of the nest.

The gun jerked as he squeezed the trigger.

An instant later the heads of the three baby birds

4

rose on straining necks. The beaks were opened wide, blindly seeking food.

"Think of it!" Wilford gloated, dropping a worm into each beak. "You've seen the miracle gun with your own eyes! Think of what a gun like this can do for the starving young birds of the world!"

Wilford straightened. The heads of the baby birds disappeared into the nest.

"This gun is the invention of my close friend, Dr. Hans Schnipplehauser of Germany. I'm his man in America," Wilford said. "I'll sell thousands of these guns to bird lovers, cities, states, and nations. But I need money to build a factory."

"How much will it cost us?" Betty Anders demanded.

"Five dollars each," Wilford answered. "For a measly five dollars, every one of my friends can buy a share. When we start selling the guns, you'll be paid back a thousand times, a hundred thousand times!"

The crowd hung back uncertainly—until the big blond boy stepped forward.

"I thought you were blowing steam, but you proved the gun works," he said to Wilford. "Here's ten bucks. I'll take two shares. You're going to make me a bundle."

His confidence in the gun chased away any doubt. The other children took out their money and hurried to form a line.

"Save your money," Encyclopedia told them. Then he explained how Wilford had tricked them. The children walked away in disgust.

Back at the detective agency, Sally Kimball admitted, "Wilford had me fooled. I thought his ray gun really worked."

"The whole meeting was sort of wacky—saving birds in a garbage dump," Encyclopedia said.

Suddenly Sally's face lit up.

"Encyclopedia," she said, "you ought to start a collection of wacky but true stories about the outdoors."

Encyclopedia walked to the shelves on the back wall of the detective agency.

"Don't tell me!" Sally gasped. "You've already started collecting wacky outdoor stories!"

Encyclopedia nodded. Sally had seen his scrapbooks of wacky, true stories about crimes, sports, spies, cars, and animals. He pulled down a yellow scrapbook she had not read. He opened it on the office desk.

"Wacky outdoors," he said.

Sally turned to the first page. . . .

For the solution to "The Case of the Invisible Ray Gun," turn to page 101.

I

How to Catch 'Em Without Hardly Trying

Watch out for stop signs. Alma Allred looked down and beheld a rainbow trout swimming along State Street in downtown Salt Lake City in 1983.

He snatched up the fish and took it to his nearby office, placed it in a basin of water, and called his mother. She thought he was teasing.

"I knew I had to get some pictures before anyone would believe me," he said.

The 13½-inch trout hadn't swum into the city to window-shop.

A five-block stretch of State Street had been sand-bagged into a canal to divert floodwater through the downtown section. The trout, which came from a rain-swollen creek in the area, had obviously made a wrong turn somewhere.

Where the flying fishes play. Londoner Roy Langdon had a free fish dinner delivered to his home after a heavy rain in 1984. The fish, four flounders, three whitings, and five smelts, fell from the sky.

Experts who know about non-flying flying fish said a freak wind was responsible. The wind had scooped the fish from the River Thames five miles away and dumped them on a patch of paving stones in Langdon's backyard.

Langdon said he would have had even more fish to fry if his cat hadn't spotted the delivery before he did.

Holy pickerel. Frankie Tate, 5, grew tired of skating on Blackbird Pond in Westerly, Rhode Island, in 1938. He cut a hole in the ice and dipped a hand in the water to sample the temperature.

"Yeow!" he yelped, and pulled out his hand—with an eight-inch pickerel hanging on to his forefinger.

That evening Frankie had a bandaged finger to show, a fish story to tell, and the pickerel to eat for supper.

Fish-in-one. James Sinclair got his fish with a golf ball.

Vacationing in Coral Gables, Florida, in 1937, Sinclair topped a shot on the seventh hole of the Miami Biltmore course. The ball sped toward a creek just as a playful mullet leapt above the surface. The ball struck the fish behind the gills. It dropped back, stunned. Sinclair "reeled" it in with his sand wedge.

Three little fishes in an itty bitty pond. In the hard times of 1932, putting a line in the water helped put food on the table.

A coolish, cloudy day in March found Mrs. James Kiser sitting on the bank of a pond near her home in Norman Park, Georgia. Mrs. Kiser was hoping to relieve the grocery budget with a trout dinner.

After two hours all she had caught was a small perch. She left it in the water at the end of her pole for a moment to drink some coffee from a thermos.

To her astonishment, the pole shot out into the pond.

Jumping into a boat, she gave pursuit. After some strenuous rowing, she recovered the pole. At the end of the line was not one fish but *three*.

A small trout had swallowed the perch. In turn, the

10

trout had been attacked by a much larger trout, a five-pounder. The first trout was too big for the second trout to swallow. Its fins, however, had acted as a hook that held the larger fish fast.

Bonito Muscle-ini. When they call the fishermen's role of honor in that great pond up in the sky, let not Harrison Outerbridge of Bermuda be overlooked.

Outerbridge made history of sorts in 1935.

A bonito took his line and yanked him overboard.

Outerbridge held on to the rod and swam back to his boat towing the fish. He was coughing seawater and struggling over the gunwale when the bonito, a no-quit fighter, jerked the rod out of his hand.

Outerbridge was a fighter, too, if a soaking wet and weary one. He was not to be bested. He dived into the water, recovered rod and fish, and lay down in his boat, completely spent.

That's when he had a good look at the size of his adversary. The monster that had been manhandling him weighed all of five pounds!

Arms and the man. For years George Bradfield of Shawnee, Oklahoma, had heard stories of the fabulous quail hunting over in Missouri. In 1939, he packed up his gear and made the trip to find out for himself.

He might as well have left his gun at home.

In the woods near Edina he flushed a covey of quail. The birds flew straight at him. Bradfield didn't have time to get off a round before the quail were overhead. In the low flurry of wings he heard the voice of opportunity.

He shot up an arm and caught a bird with his bare hand.

Catch as catch can. Some people are content merely to tell a joke, but not Lee Sisson. He invented one.

Sisson designs lures for a major American bait company. In the spring of 1984, he decided to create a joke lure and give it to a friend, Richard Price, a marlin angler.

Sisson began with an empty red-and-white aluminum cola can, which he filled with quick-drying plastic

12

foam. He covered the pop-top end with a steel disk. Next he drilled a hole lengthwise through the middle of the contraption.

Through the hole he ran a length of 300-pound test monofilament and tied two huge marlin hooks on one end. Finally, as a sort of punch line, he taped a foot-long red-and-white plastic-wrap skirt to the end of the can.

The comic lure was presented to Price during a fishing tournament at Chub Cay in the Bahamas. Sisson insisted that Price use it. Price, a good sport, agreed.

In the water the goofy thingamajig made a great

to-do. It sent off clouds of spray as it was trolled along the edge of a drop-off where marlin are regularly caught.

Suddenly, as Price's boat made a turn, a dark shape loomed behind the can-lure. Line poured from Price's reel as the can disappeared into the depths.

Price caught the fish, a 31½-pound black grouper. It was the first fish ever to fall for a joke with the response, "Okay, I'll bite."

That's reely gratitude. Lefty Kreh, a nationally known fly-fisherman, generously volunteered to take a visting outdoor writer fishing in Florida Bay in 1977.

Kreh wanted the visitor to have all the excitement, so he didn't do much fishing himself. He stood in the stern of his skiff in the hot sun and quietly poled into casting range of school after school of redfish. Only occasionally did he pick up his rod and cast.

Fishing was good. By the end of the day, Kreh's cooler bulged with redfish.

Back at the dock, the visiting writer admired the catch. Turning to the tired Kreh, he said, "I thought you were supposed to be *the* great fisherman. Why, I caught five fish to your one!"

Fish are jumpin', and the livin' ain't easy. William L. Kirst and Albert Wild were trolling in Lake Erie in 1937 when their copper lines became snarled in the propeller of their outboard motor.

As they tilted the motor to free the lines, a twelve-

15

pound sturgeon swirled up to take a bite out of the shining blades. The fish was all speed and terrible aim.

It missed the propeller, sailed clean out of the water, and landed in Kirst's lap.

Lest the fish depart by the same route, the two men jumped on it and subdued it.

"That's all there was to it," Kirst said when they came to the dock. "Here's your fish, without a hook mark on him, and now bring on your lie detector."

II

Man's Best Friends, Usually

Simply shocking. Electricity is used by some handlers to train dogs by remote control. The dog wears a collar that is operated electrically by push buttons. When the dog refuses to obey an order, it receives a mild shock.

Most dogs accept the shock as only gentle persuasion from their owners. Occasionally, though, there is a dog, such as Old Kentuck, that considers it a terrible punishment.

Bird dogs can acquire the bad habit of chasing rabbits, and Old Kentuck lost several field trials in Georgia because he abandoned his work to do just that.

So Old Kentuck's handler began to train the dog with an electric collar. After a time he was asked whether the collar was working out.

"Oh, Old Kentuck stopped chasing rabbits," the

trainer said, "but now it's pretty embarrassing at a field trial. Whenever Old Kentuck sees a rabbit, he rolls over and howls."

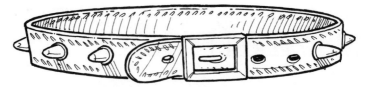

Mum's the word. Mynah birds all look exactly alike and are born copycats. They can be taught to repeat words as easily as a parrot. A Southern fish-camp operator had two mynahs, and he used their ability to mimic as a practical joke.

One of the birds could repeat many sentences, the other just one. When a fisherman entered the camp office, only the gabby bird was there. It started talking shop immediately: "Want to know where the bass are?" "I know where they're hitting." "Use a topwater plug."

The amazed angler would dash outside to fetch his buddies so they could listen to the talking bird. As soon as he was gone, the camp operator would substitute the other mynah for the gabber. The second bird beaked its single sentence only on cue.

When the excited fisherman returned with his friends, they received the silent treatment. The duped fisherman took a lot of razzing over the talking bird.

The men would start to leave, the cue for the silent mynah to sing out the only words it had learned: "Don't you know birds don't talk!"

Hare's a switch. Pocket beagles are aptly named. The dogs are so small, they usually fit into the game pockets of hunting jackets.

Bill Smith was particularly proud of his tiny beagle, Pep. He claimed Pep was spunky, and one of the best snowshoe hare-chasers around. To prove his words, he took Pep and some friends to a swampy area near Peacham, Vermont, in 1964, and turned the dog loose.

Within minutes the beagle started yapping. It had spotted an unusually large hare and was chasing it. Smith and his friends were standing on a road overlooking the swamp and could see the hare coming. Pep, barking steadily, was about fifty yards behind.

Then, in a second, the roles changed.

As if to say, "Why am I running from this shrimp?" the hare bounded behind a bush and squatted down. When the pursuing Pep was about even with the bush, the big hare bounded out.

Pep's yaps turned to yipes. The shocked dog headed for the road. When they crossed it, the hare was chasing the dog.

Bill Smith's bragging days were over.

The hand is quicker than the whistle. The competition at Vermont coon-dog trials includes what is called a "line" contest.

During this test of raccoon-hunting dogs, a drag (sometimes a bag scented with oil of anise, sometimes a wet burlap sack filled with raccoon manure) is pulled around a course roughly half a mile long. At the end

of the course two stakes are set up about thirty feet apart. To be a winner, a hound must follow the stinky trail and finish by running between the stakes.

Geoffrey Herkheimer's big black-and-tan hound was a frequent winner in the line competition. Herkheimer would show up for the trial whistling confidently—and he continued to whistle throughout the events.

A judge at the 1951 trials became suspicious. He asked Herkheimer if his whistling had anything to do with his dog's success.

The jig was up. Since Herkheimer could not deny his clandestine coaching, he admitted it. With a sly wink and a big grin, he confessed, "Yep."

Herkheimer always stood well back from the stakes, as required. He had trained his dog to come to him with a whistle pitched so high that only a dog could hear it.

Occasionally, Herkheimer put his hand to his mouth during his long spells of whistling. Only when he wanted his dog to come to him, however, did he blow the whistle concealed in his palm.

The dog would come running at top speed, straight through the stakes.

He should have smelled a rat. Scientists have held that dogs can't reason. Dog owner Charles Waterman disagrees. Not only can dogs reason, Waterman maintains, they possess a sense of humor to boot.

Waterman had a fun-loving Brittany spaniel named Kelly, who, he insists, was a practical joker.

In the fall of 1969, Waterman and Kelly came upon

the remains of a wagon in a Montana prairie. Grass and weeds had grown up through the rotting body and wheels, making it a good place to find game birds such as partridge.

Kelly circled the wagon, moved closer, and pointed. Waterman walked up, and when nothing flew from the wagon, he kicked it smartly.

Something, though not a partridge, was living in the wagon. Waterman staggered backward. A skunk had hit him with a perfectly aimed squirt.

Waterman looked around to see how his dog had fared. He spotted Kelly thirty yards away, behind a bush. The spaniel had fled when Waterman drew back his leg to deliver the kick.

"His tongue lolled from his mouth," said Waterman, "and now I know that dogs laugh."

Monkey shines. The report swept the Canarsie Bay area in New York City early in August, 1936. Someone had caught seventy-five bluefish between six and eight pounds each on the previous Saturday. The bay had not been blessed with such a bounty since the motorboat invaded its waters.

Aglow with the dream of a bucketful of blues, Billy Ray went forth in a rowboat. Accompanying him were his 16-year-old niece, Marjorie Dillon, and Jack White.

Along, too, was a pet rhesus monkey named Chico. She sat in the bow looking bored, as the humans caught weakfish. Nary a tasty blue swallowed their bait.

Chico began expressing her objections by jabbering

away. To quiet her down, Ray gave her a line to play with.

Aping Ray's skill, Chico pulled up a weakfish.

Ray leaned over to unhook the fish—and received a smack across the cheek from Chico's paw. The monkey was screaming in pain.

While catching a fish with her paws, Chico had also caught a crab with her tail. Despite her frenzied screaming and hopping, the crab hung on.

After a bit of a chase, Ray seized the dripping tail and unclamped its tormentor. There was nothing more to do but speed for shore and proclaim Chico the champion of long-tailed fishermen.

Time and again, Ray would describe to tireless listeners the thrill of fishing with a partner who could catch 'em front, back, and bare-tailed.

He gave a hoot. John La Pradd is known in South Florida as the Owl Man.

When La Pradd takes himself to cypress stands or hardwood hammocks and cuts loose with his lifelike owl imitations, the night hunters converge from all directions.

The owls believe La Pradd is one of them. The sight of him doesn't put them off. Having dropped in, they stick around for a session of stimulating conversation.

Normally, the owls chatter from the safety of a tree limb. There was one owl, though, that got too close and nearly went too far.

While demonstrating his knack to fellow outdoors-

men in 1973, La Pradd attracted an owl from miles away. La Pradd was in top form. He hooted, and the owl replied. Little by little, the sounds of the real owl drew closer. It settled in a tree directly over the men.

La Pradd continued the hooting conversation. He removed his cap and waved it at the curious bird. The owl took the gesture as an invitation to roost smack on La Pradd's balding head. It swooped down and slashed his scalp with four sharp talons.

Although bleeding and uncomfortable, La Pradd refused to brush the owl from his head. Presently, as if realizing it was hurting him, the owl hopped off and stood at his feet. Man and owl chattered away.

It was a rare sight—a wild owl, with its inborn fear of humans, positioned defenselessly on the ground in the midst of a group of men and making friendly conversation.

The owl felt safe in the company of South Florida's Owl Man. And it was.

Watt a turnoff. A four-foot pine snake was only looking for a light snack when it gobbled two electric bulbs in 1986.

Despite the double lump under its skin, it slithered across the front yard of Lynn and Carman Clark near Gainesville, Florida.

The Clarks had dumped burned-out light bulbs near their chicken coop, and they guessed what had happened. The snake had mistaken the bulbs for eggs.

The bulb-bellied reptile was taken to the Veterinary

School at the University of Florida. During a forty-five-minute operation, doctors successfully removed two fifteen-watt bulbs.

"His future looks very bright," commented Dr. Randy Caligiuri.

III

The Outdoors and the Law

Quit grousing. Trigger-happy bird hunters in the north woods of Wisconsin have learned a shooting lesson. A bird on the road might mean the law in the bush.

Wildlife officers posed stuffed grouse along paved roads in 1983. Then they lay in wait, often with video cameras, to snare violators of a hunting law. In the first two weeks, nearly thirty hunters who had leveled lead at the decoy were arrested.

Under Wisconsin law, a hunter can be fined up to $100 for firing a gun from a paved road.

Gary Scovel, a Department of Natural Resources warden, said it had been almost impossible to stop the practice until the department tried the stuffed-grouse trick.

None of the hunters who were arrested pleaded innocent.

"The basic reaction," said Scovel, "was embarrassment and shame. We've seen some red faces out there."

Target malpractice. An 18-year-old Massachusetts youth wasn't having much success hunting ducks in a marsh in 1984. So he took some target practice, shooting at a bottle lying on the ground.

He missed, and his shotgun pellets hit and slightly wounded a game warden who was hiding in the bushes.

A judge fined the youth $100 and ordered him to attend the warden's classes on hunting safety.

Heron felon. Even if goldfish don't look like your ordinary cow or hog, in England the law says they're livestock.

A judge in Birmingham ruled that a home insurance policy didn't cover fifty-seven goldfish that a hungry heron swiped from a pond.

The owner of the goldfish, Frederick Parsons, claimed he was owed £320 (then worth $384) under his home insurance policy. He argued that the stolen goldfish were personal effects, like a garden chair or a lawn mower.

The judge said, nope, goldfish are livestock and aren't covered by home insurance.

Parsons, a lawyer, didn't appeal the 1984 decision. "It's cost me about £500 ($600) already," he said. "That's more than the fish are worth."

The wily heron left him with six fish in his pond and a mite of consolation.

"That heron probably died from stuffing itself on so many of my goldfish," he said hopefully.

How to make an electric eel. Anglers in Tifton, Georgia, used their automobiles to catch fish in 1938.

They fastened a naked wire to a spark plug and dangled the other end in the water. The engine was raced, generating sufficient electricity to knock nearby fish unconscious with the shock.

The anglers got a bigger shock. Lenox Henderson, the area game warden, presented their names to the grand jury.

Hooked lines and sinkers. Hunters and fishermen have been known to wriggle desperately to avoid being hooked with fines for failing to have licenses.

Game warden Lowell Thomas caught a fisherman without a license trolling on Maine's Lobster Lake.

"I'm not fishing," the man said.

So why the lure on the end of the line?

"Oh," said the man. "The lure is there only to provide weight. I've got a new line, and I'm dragging it behind the boat to straighten it out."

Another twist to the lame-excuse game was offered by a father whom Thomas found sitting on a pier at Pemaquid Pond with his 5-year-old daughter.

The father said he didn't need a license because he was only teaching his daughter how to fish.

How come two rods?

"I'm teaching my daughter how to fish with two rods," the father explained.

A game warden in New Mexico checked out two hunters and discovered that only one of them had a hunting license.

The fast-draw excuse: "My buddy asked me to come along, and I brought the gun for self-protection."

A West Virginia hunter was equally imaginative when he was caught with a gun in one hand, a squirrel in the other, and no hunting license in his pocket.

Said he, "My grandmother is sick and dying, and she can't eat anything but squirrel."

Turned out there was no dying grandmother. If there had been, she'd have died of overeating. The hunter and his pal had bagged forty-eight squirrels.

A variation on the sympathy-seeking excuse was tried by a woman angler. She was questioned by Mississippi wildlife officers Phillip Strong and Herbert Deaton.

She had a rod and reel but no license. Nevertheless, she stoutly maintained she wasn't fishing.

"I'm a nurse," she said. "I was only helping out a friend who has heart trouble."

Anything to dodge a fine.

Joe Bland, a Kentucky game warden, was handed a tattered corner of what a fisherman claimed was his fishing license. The story: "My dog ate the rest."

And a hard-driving excuse was tried by an Ohio angler. He didn't have a license, he admitted, but he did have a learner's permit.

Follow that opossum! The guards at the Pennsylvania County jail were puzzled. The inmates had developed a keen interest in watching an opossum.

Criminals rarely get deeply involved in the study of nature. The guards began watching the inmates watch the opossum.

They soon solved the mystery. The opossum lived outside the jail. Yet daily it found its way in and *out*.

The inmates were looking for the same exit.

You light up my life. The two Georgia hunters were nervous one evening in 1979. They had been following a deer's trail for more than three hours. Now they were on land whose owners were hard on people who trespassed, and harder still on people who hunted while trespassing.

Not long after dark, the hunters' nervousness turned to downright fear. A bright light shone through the woods in their direction. They had been spotted!

They ran, scrambling and lurching, tearing their clothes and scratching their skin on branches and briars.

The light remained trained on them. Each time they looked back, it seemed to have grown larger and brighter.

They reached the barbed-wire fence that surrounded the property and crawled under it. Then they ran another hundred yards before daring to halt and look back again.

The terrible, all-knowing light was still on them!

One of the hunters, his fears quieted at reaching safety, took a long, unhurried look.

"It's the rising moon!" he exclaimed in relief.

"I *thought* that fellow with the beam was an awfully tall dude," his companion said.

Really cool. A 15½-pound rainbow trout was held in the jail in Niagara County, New York, awaiting trial for two years.

No, its constitutional rights weren't violated.

The fish actually was kept in the jail's freezer to preserve it as evidence. The case involved John Pundt, who had entered the trout in a fishing contest, the 1981 Niagara County Trout and Salmon Derby.

The county attorney argued that the fish was not eligible because it had a puncture mark near a gill. He said the mark meant the fish could have been illegally snagged. But a taxidermist testified it had been caught legally and fairly.

The jury agreed with the taxidermist. In 1983, Pundt was awarded his first prize: a powerboat, trailer, and equipment worth $25,000.

Down the hatch. Fish in New York's Ellicott Creek went on a paralyzing binge in 1933.

Huge numbers of them ended up floating stiffly on the surface. Game wardens hauled some to fresh water,

where they slowly wriggled back to consciousness.

Their behavior suggested a fishy version of a hangover. An investigation led to zealous federal government agents finding an illegal still. One thousand gallons of intoxicating mash had been dumped into the creek.

Honestly, it's the best policy. Charles W. Rushing of Mendenhall, Mississippi, caught nineteen crappies in 1985. One of them tested his honesty.

Rushing was home before he noticed among his catch a fish with a tag. On the tag was printed "big" followed by a dollar sign.

He called back to Pelahatchie Bay where he had been fishing. "They told me what I had caught, and to hurry up and get that fish up there alive," he said.

Good news and bad awaited him.

He had caught one of the eight winning fish in a contest in which the prizes ranged from $2,000 to $25,000. The prize for his fish was a completely outfitted fishing boat, motor, and trailer. Total value: $5,000.

That was the good news. The bad news was that since he had not purchased the four-dollar Bounty Hunter Badge, his fish did not qualify for the contest.

"I had to tell the truth," said Rushing, an unemployed lumber-mill worker and the father of three. "There ain't no other way."

Because he was a true sportsman, tournament director Harry Stressel awarded him $100.

"It's not everyone who would admit up front that his

catch wasn't legal," Stressel said. "We've had people try to cheat in the past, and we caught them."

Down by the ol' nil stream. Can tractors catch fish? The answer is yes. Unlawfully.

Rangers of the Georgia Wild Life Division came upon 2,000 pounds of bass, bream, and jack that had been shoveled from a pond near Douglas in 1939. A huge tractor-operated pump had first drained the pond as dry as a fish market.

Six men were arrested, charged with illegal farming . . . er, fishing.

There's a lot of buck in that doe. Richard A. Bauman of Gloucester, Massachusetts, illegally shot a female deer during the 1955 buck season. Game commission officials let him get away with it. Bauman had made an honest mistake.

His 200-pound doe looked like a buck. It had a full set of antlers, the first ever reported on a female in the white-tailed deer population.

IV

Making the Best of It

Put up your dukes. Roughing it in the wilds—cooking on a camp fire, sleeping on a bedroll—is fun to most hunters. But not to all hunters. Take, if you can, Grand Duke Alexander, son of the Czar of Russia.

In 1872, the duke traveled to Nebraska to hunt buffalo. "Roughing it" was the last thing on his mind.

With him went several railroad cars, including two sleepers, a dining car, and a refrigerator car stocked with grouse, quail, and other assorted goodies.

Nothing but the best for Grand Duke Alexander. His guide was General Phillip Sheridan of Civil War fame. Helping out were George Custer, Buffalo Bill Cody, and 1,000 Sioux Indians.

Scant comfort. It was almost dark when Bill Hallstrom, his wife, Gwen, and their two young children arrived at Indiana's scenic Brown County Park in 1977.

The fast-disappearing daylight made it impossible for the family to search for a cozy campsite—one located near the water or in a forest clearing. They put up their tent alongside a trail that seemed to run through the park.

After the family had eaten their dinner of leftover chicken, rolls, and cole slaw, they crawled onto their cots and went to sleep.

Early the next morning they were awakened by the sounds of trotting horses and laughing riders. The trail near which they had pitched their tents was actually a riding path and the source of the horselaughs.

In the dark the Hallstroms had pitched their tent on a pile of dry manure that had been swept from the trail.

Cold duck, anyone? Mike Pearson, manager of an animal shelter in Bedford Township, Michigan, received the call on a bitter-cold December day in 1983. The caller had seen two ducks stuck in a frozen pond a hundred feet offshore.

Pearson rushed to the rescue. Bravely he waded into the pond until the ice could support him. He crawled to within arm's length of the sick-looking ducks.

That's when he discovered they weren't so sick as they were wooden—a pair of wooden decoys.

Henry and Henrietta found a home in the animal shelter as trophies of Pearson's dedication.

Fail safe. Leland Burroughs of Interlachen, Florida, knows a preacher who would have hired an armed guard to protect a bass he had caught.

Burroughs and the preacher were fishing in the latter's new $12,000 bass boat on Rodman Reservoir in northern Florida.

They'd fished only a short time when an enormous bass hit the preacher's lure. The preacher worked the big fish near the boat. Burroughs lifted it out of the water and tossed it onto the deck.

For a minute or so the preacher just sat there, stone-like, gawking at the fourteen-pound lunker.

Now, to understand what happened next, it is important to know something about the preacher's fishing luck. It was rotten. For one reason or another he had lost so many big bass that he thought failure was his guide.

The preacher awoke from his trance and sprang into action. He opened one of his boat's storage compartments, tossed in the bass, closed the lid, and secured it with a padlock.

"Let's go," he commanded.

Burroughs obediently cranked up the motor and headed back to the boat ramp.

When the boat was safely on the trailer, Burroughs asked the preacher why he had quit fishing so early, and why he had locked up the bass.

"That's the biggest bass I've ever seen," explained the preacher. "I got what I came for."

"Why the lockup?" Burroughs inquired.

"Well," said the preacher, "if we had hit a log or something on the way back and the boat sank, I still could go back and retrieve my bass from the locked compartment. If the fish were in the unlocked live-well and we sank, it would have been just another one that got away."

Trout-of-bounds. There's more than one way to catch a fish.

Bob Brannum, basketball coach at Vermont's Norwich University, and Perk Angwin, fishing editor of a local newspaper, proved the old saying conclusively.

The day after the two friends returned from a trout-fishing excursion, Angwin got a telephone call from the athletic director at Norwich.

"Did Brannum really catch that big rainbow trout he's showing off around here?" he asked.

Angwin replied truthfully, "I saw him catch it."

Angwin and Brannum had been fishing in a private pond crowded with brook trout and a few very large rainbows.

"Wish we could catch one of those big rainbows," Brannum said.

Angwin, who knew the habits of the fish, changed flies. He hooked and landed a 6½-pound rainbow on his next cast.

"I'd sure like to take that one to Norwich and show it to some of my friends," Brannum remarked wistfully.

"Here," said Angwin, and tossed the fish.

Brannum, a former Boston Celtic basketball player, deftly caught it.

Light reading. An outdoor survival book saved two youths stranded on a ledge in Bells Canyon, Utah, in 1985.

They remained on the ledge, just as the book instructed. They built a lean-to and tried to light a fire with twigs to signal rescuers. After two hours and most of their matches, they said to heck with it and burned the book, *Outdoor Survival Skills*. The flames were spotted about midnight, and the youths were picked up by a helicopter.

Drop everything. Frank O. Hill of Union, South Carolina, had money problems in 1975. His quail business was going under because of rising feed bills.

Until he noticed what the rest of us have been missing: "How beautiful a quail dropping is."

He embedded a dropping in clear plastic. Encased, it looked even better than in the raw. It was definitely more fun to hold. He made a tie tack out of it.

Some friends admired the creation. Encouraged, Hill began making other jewelry.

"I found that I could sell a quail egg for a dime, but the quail laid only one egg a day," he said. "I can sell the dropping in plastic for five dollars, and a quail produces about forty droppings a day."

Clearly a triumph of mind over matter.

Par for the course. To a golfer, a water hazard is a place to lose balls and strokes, something to be avoided like a double bogie or falling off a roof. To Henry Baxley, a dedicated fisherman, a water hazard was a small, inviting lake.

Normally his company held its yearly sales meeting at a lakeside resort. In 1967, however, the meeting was moved to the landlocked Doral Country Club in Miami, Florida.

The Doral is famous for its challenging Blue Demon golf course. Fishing there is for sunken golf balls and clubs hurled by hot-tempered players.

Baxley was disappointed, not discouraged. When the other sales managers headed for the course with their

47

clubs, he headed for the course with rod and reel. At the first man-made "lake" he caught a huge twelve-pound bass.

Special delivery. Conservationists had a chance to strike back at polluters in 1971.

The Bream Fisherman Association held a raffle titled "The First Annual Pollution Sweepstakes" at the Pensacola (Florida) Interstate Fair. The prize was 5,000 dead fish—to be delivered to the winner's favorite polluter.

The fish were small menhaden, which had perished during one of the summer's giant fish kills in Escambia Bay.

The dead fish were displayed in a huge bottle, in front of which was a carved tombstone with the inscription: "In Memory of Escambia Bay, Killed by Pollution."

Pollution from factories was blamed for the death of the fish and oyster population of the bay, which had once supported a large fishing industry.

Name of the game. The folks up in British Columbia, Canada, are savvy. They know what sportfishermen like to catch, and it isn't big, ugly dogfish.

A tad of brainstorming dressed up the dogfish's image with a new name: salmon shark.

In 1985, a fishing association sponsored the first salmon-shark derby. The competition doubled as a conservation project. Dogfish—now salmon shark—have

little commercial value. They eat salmon and compete with them for food.

50

Don't scream, get a pail. A sea monster was sighted at dusk in Swan Lake, Michigan, in 1946.

Reports of a horned creature with a long tail sent powerboats racing for the docks. Wide-eyed fishermen scrambled ashore. Panic cleared the lake within minutes.

The "sea monster" proved to be a black cow. After a cooling swim, bossy wandered back to the Carl Ferris farm mooing contentedly.

V

Lady Luck Can Laugh

Eating fish can be harmful to your health. No one will ever know why the fisherman opened his mouth, only that his timing was awful.

The fisherman, a villager in Malay, had been drawing in his net in a rice field. As he looked over his catch, a fish leapt out of the water and disappeared down his throat.

The British Medical Journal, which reported the incident in 1947, stated that the fisherman was taken to the hospital within the hour.

At first a doctor tried to pull out the fish (a six-inch Ikan Betok) by using forceps. He grasped the tail, but it came off. The rest of the intruder had to be "delivered" in the operating theater.

The fish went the way of all fish out of water. The patient recovered.

Look, Ma, no fish. By 1984, the annual ice-fishing tournament in Cottonwood, Minnesota, was known as the Fishless Derby.

Nobody caught a fish—for the twenty-second year in a row.

Sacrificial calf. Ernest Hemingway hated sharks. Not only did they occasionally attack people, but they frequently stole game fish from his fishing line.

While he was fishing off Key West, Florida, his hatred of sharks reached new heights.

He blamed a shark for shooting him.

He had hooked a mako shark. As he fought the man-

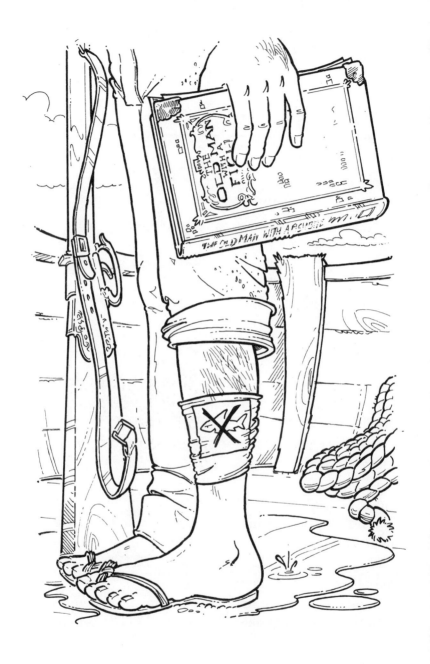

eater, he got out the only gun he had aboard—a 22-caliber automatic pistol.

When the mako finally was at boatside, Hemingway raised it with a gaff hook and turned its head in order to shoot it in the brain.

The wild twisting of the shark broke the gaff. The shaft struck Hemingway in his gun hand, causing him to jerk the trigger. The gun discharged.

The bullet ricocheted off the deck and into Hemingway's muscular calf.

Back in Key West, the doctor decided to leave the bullet where it was. Removing it would require digging three or four inches into Hemingway's calf.

Hemingway carried the souvenir of the shark for the rest of his life.

Giving it both barrels. In Arizona a 23-year-old hunter shot himself in the leg in 1971. He fired his gun to summon aid and shot himself in the other leg.

Portrait of the artist. Wildlife photographers like M. Timothy O'Keefe often spend days, even weeks, in blinds waiting for their subjects to come close enough to be captured on film. When the animal does come within camera range, the shooting must take place in seconds.

When photographing birds, it is particularly important to have cameras prefocused. O'Keefe uses his driver's license. He tapes it to a branch the bird is likely to perch upon and focuses on the letters of his name.

When that is done, all there is left to do is remove the license, be alert, wait, and hope.

One night in 1979, O'Keefe was waiting in his blind when he heard an owl approaching. The bird was making a squealing sound, which told O'Keefe that it probably had caught a rodent.

It was just the picture O'Keefe wanted, one for which he had waited long and patiently.

As the bird landed, O'Keefe tripped the shutter, and his four strobe lamps filled the night with blinding light.

O'Keefe saw everything: the owl, the rodent, and, under the owl's talons, a photograph of himself.

The wildlife picture was useless. He had forgotten to untape his driver's license—with his photograph on it —after he'd focused his camera.

The real decoy. Elmer Crowell (1862–1952) of East Harwich, Massachusetts, is no longer a forgotten artist of the outdoors.

Working with a pocketknife and a rasp, Crowell carved bird decoys—mainly ducks and geese—out of wood. Occasionally his wife helped with the painting.

As late as 1922, his simple, graceful decoys were still selling for the original price, two dollars apiece. If a customer wanted a little extra detailing, the cost went up about fifty cents.

The value of Crowell's carvings climbed slowly till the 1980s. Then the price of a single decoy soared fantastically on the collectors' market—past $100,000, past \$200,000, past \$300,000. In July, 1986, one of his preening pintail ducks sold for a record \$319,000.

What's up, Doc? In the darkness before dawn, the guide was taking a group of duck hunters, including Dr. Arvid Bergman, by boat to their positions on the lake.

The Georgia fog coated the surface. Between darkness and fog, the guide became a trifle confused as to exactly where he was. But the party knew the sun would soon clear things up.

All the duck hunters wore waders. They merely had to stand in whatever shallow spot the guide chose for them and wait for the ducks.

"Dr. Bergman," said the guide, "you get out here. This is one of the best places on the lake. My son stood here yesterday and bagged his limit in less than ten minutes."

So Bergman picked up his shotgun and stepped out of the boat—and into eight feet of water.

A camouflage hat floated up first. Then the doctor appeared, sputtering in the cold.

"How tall is your boy?" he asked the guide.

One way to catch a train. Before a dam was built on the Clyde River, where it entered Lake Memphremagog near the Quebec border, there was a spring run of salmon from lake to river.

There was a run of fishermen too. They flocked to the railroad bridge at the junction of lake and river, hoping to catch their limit of fish.

Since the bridge was such a popular spot, the railroad asked the anglers to be extra careful. If they behaved, they would be allowed to continue using the bridge.

As often happens, one fisherman got careless and spoiled things for everyone.

He made a long, low back-cast as a freight train was crossing the bridge. Instead of hooking a salmon, he hooked the train's brakeman by the pants and jerked him off his feet. Fortunately, the fishing line broke. The brakeman wasn't seriously injured.

Still, the railroad reasoned that one hooked brakeman was the limit. Thereafter the bridge was closed to fishermen.

Grin, for you may have to bear it. Black bears reach 400 to 500 pounds, have huge claws, and can be deadly dangerous when angry.

When they beg for food along national park highways, their appearance is deceptive. They look friendly and tame. Tourists delight in taking pictures of them in order to relive their vacations later on.

One tourist at the 500,000-acre Great Smoky Mountains National Park in 1973 had an expensive camera and a strange sense of humor. He wanted a picture of a bear behind the steering wheel of his car.

Ignoring park rules against feeding animals, the know-it-all tourist dropped food in a trail leading from the roadside to his open car. By and by, a large beggar bear began snacking its way along the trail until it was in the driver's seat. Gleefully, the tourist slammed the door.

The plan worked well until the bear finished off the food. Abruptly, plan and car came apart.

The bear ripped the front seat, either in searching for more food or in anger at being imprisoned. It was ruining the backseat when a ranger arrived. The bear was freed to resume its hobo life.

And the tourist? He had lost his peculiar sense of humor, along with the interior of his car. He threatened to sue the park service for letting a dangerous animal roam free.

What's more, in his excitement he had forgotten to take any pictures.

Paradise lost. The tarpon that Bill Flynn and Mike Coggins caught in a shallow Gulf Coast bay was just too big to lift out of the water. They had to tip their small wooden skiff till they could half roll and half float the 100-pounder aboard.

The tarpon was less tired than the two men thought. It came to life in the boat, slamming around like a wrecking ball.

A tackle box flew into the air, scattering hooks, lures, and sinkers. A water jug, an ice chest, and both oars were shattered.

"Get out of the boat and let him have it!" Coggins shouted.

The two men jumped out of the boat and into four feet of water.

"When he quiets down, we'll get back in and take him home," Coggins remarked as one of the seats sailed past him.

A moment later the skiff's plank construction came completely apart.

The pieces drifted off, the tarpon swam away, and the two anglers sloshed forlornly back to shore.

A hull of a plug. Once upon a time, a fish copied the little Dutch boy who stuck his finger into a hole in the dike and saved the old hometown.

The steamship *Dampen* was outward-bound in 1933 when she developed an unstoppable leak. She swung around and barely managed to limp into Newport News, Virginia.

Workers at a dry-dock company pumped out the water and examined the hole in her hull.

Wedged in the hole was a shark. It had dammed most of the inflow of seawater, and without question saved the ship from sinking.

Can you top this? Chicagoan Joe Bonadona waited all year to make a trip to Costa Rica to catch tarpon and snook. During the winter he spent every spare minute hand-making the fishing rods he planned to use.

The great day finally came. Bonadona lovingly packed his rods, boarded the plane, and in due course arrived at camp. He immediately unpacked the rods and rigged them for fishing.

Bonadona was ready. He grabbed his rods, clutching three in each hand, and hurried to arrange for guides to take him out.

He rushed into the lodge where, with a clang, clatter, and *whump,* months of work and planning went up in the air. A low-hanging ceiling fan sliced the tops off all his rods.

A fish to the finish. The rules for the 1985 West Palm Beach Kiwanis Fishing Tournament were simple.

The first boat back at the dock with a wahoo, a bonito, a dolphin, and a kingfish would win the "richest one-day saltwater tournament in the southeastern United States." The prize: $50,000.

More than 200 boats from all over Florida left the Palm Beach Shores marina just before sunrise. Among

them was the *Gulf Seeker* with a four-man team of Frank Baron, Ron Gabler, Jon Vanetta, and Rozzie Marinelli.

Lady Luck tossed them a bouquet of thorns. The fish didn't get away. The prize did.

Baron caught all the fish for his team. At nine A.M., he reeled in the kingfish. Half an hour later he pulled in the wahoo. Two down, two to go! At eleven A.M., he got the dolphin and, at eleven forty-five, the bonito.

"We radioed that we had 'em all," Baron said.

Gabler pointed the *Gull Seeker* for port and gunned the engine.

Clank, whir, and misery. The transmission quit.

With only one of its two engines working, the boat struggled to the dock four minutes too late. The prize money went to the four fishermen aboard *The Shark Bait* who, with no transmission trouble, raced in at fifty miles an hour.

"A bummer," commented Baron.

Say it again. Baron, Vanetta, and Gabler worked for a transmission parts firm.

Their misery had company.

Alastair Gregor and his three daughters caught a wahoo, a dolphin, a kingfish, and a bonito in three hours—less time than the winners.

They did it in a chartered boat, as part of the yearly outing Gregor takes with his daughters before they return to their homes in Edinburgh, Scotland.

The once-a-year anglers brought in the fish on Friday, a day too soon. They knew nothing about the $50,000 tournament slated for Saturday.

Hold that line. Hugo Volkan was fishing near Hammond, Indiana, in 1931, when he had the misfortune to hook a pickerel.

In his excitement, he sprained his ankle, fell to the bottom of the boat, gashed his scalp, wrenched his back and neck in rising, lost his false teeth, and finally toppled into the water.

When pulled out by his companions, he still had a grip on his fishing pole—and the fish.

VI

Mixed Bag

Pop goes the porcupine. For a scary second, Sam Cahill, a former New England construction worker, thought someone had launched a porcupine at him. Not porcupine quills, mind you, but a whole, live porcupine.

Cahill was dozing near an earth-moving machine when he was awakened by an explosion. He opened his eyes in time to see a porcupine flying through the air.

The animal had chewed its way through a tire casing on the earth-mover. Blast-off came when the tire blew up.

After touching down, the porcupine shook its head and ambled back for some more chewing.

Thank cod! In 1984, Waldemar Andersen, a Norwegian fisherman from Oslo, returned to the spot in the North Sea where he and his wife, Ragnhild, liked to fish.

It turned into a jewel of a trip.

While cleaning the catch, Waldemar found a gold earring in the stomach of a cod.

The earring looked familiar. . . .

Ragnhild had dropped it overboard the previous week.

"Think of all the fish swimming around in the North Sea, and the same cod that swallowed my earring bit on my husband's hook," Ragnhild said. "It's completely improbable."

Never look a miffed bass in the mouth. Mark Parker, of Linden, Louisiana, caught only one fish over in Caney Lake that May afternoon in 1984. He nearly threw it back. An hour later he wished he had.

The fish was a two-pound bass, small but a fighter. Parker took it home and slid it into the kitchen sink to clean.

He stuck his finger in its mouth and was bitten.

By a snake.

Just before the bass had seized Parker's black plastic worm, it had gulped down a foot-long water moccasin. The snake was still alive and in a biting-back mood.

The bite sent Parker to the hospital. He was treated for blood poisoning and kept overnight.

From his hospital bed, he announced his intention of having the fish mounted.

"It'll make a good conversation piece," he said.

And, yes, he'd think twice before putting his hand into the mouth of another fish. Well, for a little while, anyway.

Treasure stomach. While on a fishing trip near West Stockbridge, Massachusetts, in 1935, John Fallon, Jr., lost a pouch containing a silver pocketknife and chain, his wife's wedding ring, a religious medal, and his wallet. Three years later, John Gannon boated a three-pound pickerel. Inside it were the missing treasures, all in good condition.

A time-consuming story. After eight years, John Bembers of Grand Rapids, Michigan, got his watch back.

In 1976, Bembers had lost the watch overboard while fishing in Lake Michigan. Three years passed till it turned up in the stomach of a forty-two-pound salmon caught in the lake by Thomas Kresnak.

The salmon had eaten the shiny watch, probably mistaking it for a crippled minnow.

Kresnak needed five years to track down Bembers. He succeeded with the aid of a partial inscription on the back of the watch.

Salmon oil may have lubed the workings. The watch was returned to Bembers's wrist, undigested and ticking.

Something to sink into your teeth. A group of sportfishermen were sitting around in the Tropic Star

Lodge after a day of fishing off Panama's Pacific coast, bragging and telling tall tales about big fish caught on light tackle.

Suddenly one of the anglers, Cliff Kiester, an Oklahoma oilman, blurted out, "Why, I can catch a Pacific sailfish on dental floss."

"Absurd" was the reaction. "Prove it" was the challenge.

That night Kiester spooled several hundred feet of dental floss onto his reel and confidently went to bed.

The next day the sea was alive with sailfish. Nearly everyone fishing hooked one, and they all managed to keep an eye on Kiester and his dental-floss fishing line. They expected to see him humiliated at the first strike.

Kiester amazed them. Not only did he hook a sailfish, but he worked it surely and quickly to the boat.

That evening, the doubters sheepishly asked him his secret. There must be some catch to the catch, some trick involved.

"It was easy," Kiester said. "Dental floss is stronger than the ten- to twenty-pound test monofilament lines you all are using."

A few of the diehards tugged and yanked at some dental floss. They became believers when they couldn't break it.

Quoth the raven. Leonid Germatsky of Minsk, Russia, had a pet talking raven, Karlusha, that let him know how neighboring ice-fishermen were doing. Karlusha screeched in her vocabulary of about sixty words. The

bird strutted from one ice hole to another, loudly calling out the catch.

The raven was also a slick thief. When fishermen looked the other way, she ceased yakking and swiped buttons, lighters, and fishing gear and hid them by Germatsky's fishing hole.

'Ale fellow. Louis McIntyre worked up a lusty appetite battling a 21¾-pound muskellunge for 35 minutes in 1945. When he hauled in the fish in Rhinelander, Wisconsin, he discovered his reward. He had caught not only his dinner but also a drink to wash it down with.

Inside the stomach of the fish was a bottle of beer.

A biting farewell. Theodore Roosevelt, the trust-busting president, enjoyed shooting at corrupt corporations in America as much as at lions in Africa.

Consequently, some captains of industry didn't share the enthusiasm with which the public greeted Roosevelt's every adventure. The financial giant J. P. Morgan, for one, hated him with a passion.

Less than three weeks after he left the White House, Roosevelt set out on an African safari. Thousands of well-wishers came to the dock to see him off. Morgan was pointedly absent. But he did have a biting comment about the ex-president's trip to Africa.

"America," declared Morgan, "hopes every lion will do its duty."

Thy will be done. A fish delivered a prayer in Miami,

Florida, in 1938. When John Russell landed a twelve-pound grouper, a shell on which the Lord's Prayer was engraved came out on the hook as well.

Puff, the magic rabbit. The rabbit disappeared without even the wave of a magician's wand.

Putt Kennedy, Fric Fracassi, and Harry Blundt were astounded. They were hunting in a wooded area near Chelsea, Vermont, when Blundt's dog, Ned, chased a snowshoe hare from behind a lean-to. Kennedy used the lean-to for storing dynamite and blasting powder that he needed in removing tree stumps.

The hare ran across the line of fire and vanished in a flash and a cloud of smoke.

The men rubbed their eyes and investigated. Aside from a tiny bit of white fur on a bush, there was not a trace of the hare.

The only explanation was that the hare had exploded. It had eaten some of Kennedy's stored explosives and turned itself into a hopping bomb.

One for the birds. Moviegoers who know their birdcalls can spot the giveaway in a film with a foreign setting that was actually shot in California.

In the background can be heard the Whe-*Wheee*-Whuh calls of California quails (or valley quails) chattering to each other.

California quails like the life in the Los Angeles basin, and that includes Hollywood. They delight the average bird-watcher. To sound crews on outdoor stu-

dio lots, however, they're strictly headaches.

For knowledgeable moviegoers, the call of the California quail can shatter the illusion of a film supposedly set in Spain or Italy or Texas.

Let your conscience be your guide. The Maine Warden Service, a University of Maine search-and-rescue team, and a private pilot joined forces to save three university students in 1983.

"They were in a real rough area on the back side of what people around here call Porcupine Mountain," said Richard Scribner of the University of Maine.

The three young people who were rescued were Scribner's students. They became lost while taking a test on the use of compass and map.

Lens sakes alive. Dr. Harvey Barnett, a professional wildlife photographer from Sanford, Florida, was taking pictures of birds when he was conked on the head.

The attack came for an out-of-this-world reason.

Barnett had draped a dark cloth over his head and shoulders and was hunched over his camera, which rested on a tripod. As he focused his telescopic lens, *whack!*

From out of the blue an elderly woman bird-watcher clubbed him on the noggin with her sturdy walking stick.

Barnett fell from under the dark cloth. The lady gasped and apologized. He had appeared to be wearing a space suit, she explained.

She had mistaken him for an alien invader aiming a ray gun at the unsuspecting birds.

No biz like show biz. A popular outdoor tourist attraction in Florida is the waterskiing show at Silver Springs. Lesser known is the attraction in the woods nearby—a colony of monkeys. They are the descendants of a band of monkeys that escaped during the filming of a Tarzan movie in the 1930s.

No bats in this belfry. The pinewood tower stands forgotten on Sugarloaf Key in the Florida Keys, a casualty in the war against mosquitoes.

The tower would be filled today with fat, happy bats if the plans of C. B. Perky had worked out.

Perky owned a resort on Sugarloaf Key. He built the tower in 1929 as a home for bats. He hoped they would eat mosquitoes and make the lower Florida Keys area more comfortable for fishermen and boaters.

Perky wasn't alone in his dream to rid the area of bites and buzzing.

BAT TOWER WOULD SOLVE MOSQUITO PROBLEM EVEN ON FLORIDA KEYS, stated a headline in *The South Dade News Leader* in 1928. The article added, "What a heaven on earth lower Florida would be, summer as well as winter, if there were no mosquitoes."

The article spurred Perky on. He built the tower the following year.

Alas, the tower stood but flopped. The bats never moved in.

The first load of bat bait that Perky bought to lure them into the tower was washed away by high tides. He tried to purchase more bait. None was available.

The scientist who had developed the bat bait, Dr. Charles A. Campbell of San Antonio, Texas, had died. His secret formula died with him.

Today mosquitoes, not bats, fly happily around the bat tower. It stands lonely and empty, an aging monument to itching.

How to tend your stock. P. E. Turnball, a farmer in Lee, Massachusetts, grew tired of losing cows to deer hunters year after year.

So he labeled each milker, "Don't shoot me. I am a cow." The words, in big black letters, were displayed on white blankets worn by the entire herd during the deer hunting season in 1913.

His losses that year: no cows, seven blankets.

Well, blow me down. George Riesselmann was one happy hunter in 1938. He forgot to load his gun.

Stalking through the woods near Waukegan, Illinois, he spied a rabbit sitting on a package. He aimed and squeezed. The hammer fell upon an empty chamber.

The rabbit darted away, leaving just the package.

It contained six sticks of dynamite.

Think big. You say you'd like to cruise the Caribbean in your own yacht but you can't afford it? Not to worry. Follow the example of Cecil Gates, a retired Los Angeles schoolteacher.

Gates built himself an ocean liner.

What's more, he built it at home of plywood and fiberglass. It took eight months. When he was done, he had a scaled-down model of the 882½-foot *Titanic*.

Once the world's largest—and still the most famous —steamship, *Titanic* never completed its maiden voyage. Considered "unsinkable," it struck an iceberg in the North Atlantic in 1912 and went under. About 1500 people died.

Gates's twenty-two-foot, seaworthy model of the ill-fated ship seats two, sleeps two, and carries only three life jackets. When the boat is a hundred yards offshore,

people seeing it for the first time think it is a real ocean liner—until a private cabin cruiser passes close. Then eyesight adjusts, delivering astonished viewers from the illusion of gigantic size.

The tiny *Titanic* probably attracts the most comments of any boat in California waters. Jokers can't resist shouting, "Watch out for icebergs!"

Fishermen's dozen. A fish that had a right to claim the title "Toughest in the Nation" was finally taken in 1941.

Marcell Wackenie, angling in Indian Lake, Tennessee, pulled in the large spoonbill catfish. It had fourteen hooks in its mouth.

Shipwrecked. Until Jim Wilcox caught his record tarpon in 1985, no one bothered with an offbeat statistic: the time it takes to land a fish.

Wilcox, his buddy Bill Snow, and their guide, Fred Woodward, were fishing the incoming tide for speckled trout at the mouth of the Folly River at Doboy Sound, Georgia. Around six P.M., a trout, medium-sized, took Wilcox's bait.

Wilcox began reeling in the fish on a thirty-six-pound test braided nylon line when a splash and a silver form hit. A huge tarpon leaped out of the water with the trout in its mouth.

Wilcox, in a reflex action, tugged the line taut, and a 6-foot-¾-inch 142-pound tarpon flipped itself into the boat and thrashed madly about.

"Now, the boat was just eighteen feet long," said Wilcox, "and, brother, we gave the fellow seventeen. We were ready to give it all eighteen. For a while there we thought it was going to sink us."

The big tarpon flung itself from bow to stern, tearing up everything in its way. Seats were ripped from their bolts, poles flew overboard, the boat top was shredded, and the trim destroyed.

For at least half an hour Wilcox, Snow, and Woodward perched anxiously on the rear of the boat as the tarpon did $1,000 worth of damage. When it quieted down, they took it to the marina and weighed it unofficially at the rod and gun club. It looked to be a record catch.

Elated, they winched the fish into a pickup truck and

drove to Darien and Thompson's Seafood, which had a calibrated scale.

The fish weighed almost five pounds more than the state-record 137-pound 8-ounce tarpon caught in 1969. Moreover, Wilcox had landed it in five seconds, plainly a world bite-to-boat mark for big-game fish.

"Everybody's been telling me to make up a fish story," said Wilcox, "to say I played him three, four hours, and rassled him into the boat. Heck, don't you think the truth is pretty close to being enough?"

VII

Tall Tales

The sky's the limit when American outdoorsmen get together to swap tall tales. Here are just a few.

In South Florida they tell about the two mosquitoes that left their home in a mangrove forest. The mosquitoes flew out over the water and lifted a fisherman from his boat.

As they bore him off, one mosquito said to the other, "Should we eat him here or carry him back into the mangroves?"

"We'd better eat him here," the other answered. "If we take him into the mangroves, the big fellows might steal him from us."

In the north woods mosquitoes are sizable too. Out of

Washington comes the yarn of the hunter who saw a mosquito so big, he had to shoot it with a rifle. He brought down the mosquito—and the eagle it was carrying.

An Ozark farmer's constant companion was a droopy, slow-moving hound. No one had ever seen it break into a run.

Its owner, nonetheless, was forever talking up the hound's fitness, speed, and great hunting skills. "Best coon-catching dog in the state," he bragged.

One day a cousin from the other side of the mountain came to visit the farmer. While the two men were lazing on the porch, three raccoons dashed by. The dog merely wrinkled its nose.

"Look at him sitting there, will you?" scoffed the cousin. "Coon dog, my hat!"

"Hah!" chortled the farmer. "He knows them. Just you wait till a strange coon comes by here!"

R. C. Cross of Wausau, Wisconsin, tells of catching fish by pouring hair tonic into a stream. He then sets a barber pole on the bank and shouts, "Next!" The fish jump out of the water.

Fifty years before the government ruled that tobacco was harmful, Nantucket fishermen were catching tobacco-chewing cod.

The fishermen simply threw quids of tobacco into the water where the nicotine-nutty cod gathered. The fish took the tobacco and chewed. When they swam to the surface to spit, the fishermen scooped them in with a net.

Pistol Pete Fallowfield caught a pickerel while fishing in Hogs Run, a lake in Maine. He was bending over to admire the fish when a silver dollar fell out of his pocket. The fish swallowed the coin, flipped out of the canoe, and swam away.

Two years later Pistol Pete was fishing in the same spot and caught the same pickerel. He remembered his lost silver dollar. When he opened the fish, he found the dollar, along with three pennies and a nickel—two years of interest on his money.

A fellow down in Georgia liked to fish early. One morning he hiked to the pond before the sun rose, tramping through fog so thick he could barely see six inches in front of his nose. He stopped and cast where he thought the pond was and got five bass, one right after the other. Then the fog lifted, and he saw that he hadn't been fishing in the pond at all. The doggone bass had floated out of the lake and were swimming around in the thick fog, gobbling swarms of mosquitoes. He allowed that you don't see fog like that anymore.

A Virginia game warden was rocking on his front porch when a stranger approached. He must have been staying at the hotel; he was all duded up to go fishing. And he was worried. Somebody'd told him that to catch

a trout legally in Virginia, it had to be six inches long. Because he didn't have a measuring tape, the warden sawed a stick exactly six inches for him, and he went off full of mustard. Four hours later he came back—without a single trout. Sort of surprising, because the lake was full of 'em. The warden said, "Funny you didn't get any fish." And the dude said, mighty sad, "I caught a lot, but they were either under or over six inches. I had to throw 'em all back."

Trappers in the old Pacific Northwest were renowned as one tough breed of men.

Take the case of the burly young man who rode into Rat's Hole. Even in a town accustomed to men proving their toughness, the young man attracted attention. He sat astride a full-grown grizzly bear. For a hat he wore a roped mountain lion, and in his hand squirmed a rattlesnake, which he used as a whip.

He limped into a saloon and growled, "Give me a glass of carbolic acid and some kerosene for a chaser."

The bartender served the drinks and asked the young man where he was from.

"Been trapping up in the hills," he said, "but the tough guys chased me out."

In the bitter cold of the Arctic, a young Eskimo hunter named Schlomowitz was going through the manhood ritual. He had passed the tests of torture and hunger. Now he had to perform the final feat: slaying a polar bear.

A blizzard struck, and Schlomowitz lost his way. After half an hour of aimless wandering, he encountered a savage polar bear. The young hunter reached for his gun, an old muzzle-loading musket. To his horror, he discovered that he had plenty of powder but no bullets.

The bear faced him and snarled viciously. Schlomowitz retreated. Fear caused his brow to bead with perspiration. In the sub-zero air, the beads froze instantly.

Using the beads as bullets, the quick-thinking youth loaded his gun and fired. The charging bear dropped dead at his feet.

A Canadian had been fishing all day without any luck. He was puffing on his pipe and thinking of rowing back to camp when a duck settled on the water near him. To his amazement, the duck began diving every four or five seconds.

After giving this curious behavior several minutes of study, the fisherman solved the mystery. The duck mistook his pipe puffs for the puffs of smoke from a gun barrel.

The pipe was puffed faster and harder. The duck dived deeper and stayed down longer. After a while, the smoking pipe could keep the duck submerged for quite long periods.

Finally, the fishless fisherman got his dinner. He puffed with all the strength left in his lungs. The duck stayed under till it drowned.

Out in Colorado an old-timer knows a lake that's the next best thing to paradise. The fish bite so furiously, he has to duck into his cabin to bait his hook.

And let's not forget to mention the man in Texas who measures his fish only between the eyes.

Or the Iowa farmer who hauled a giant bass from his pond. The water rushed down so far and made the mill run backward so fast, it put fifty bushels of corn right back onto the cob.

Granny Dobson was a little old lady with a sharp business sense. Her dry-goods store in North Carolina prospered, and she made regular trips to Boston to buy merchandise at the best prices.

In 1903, she took the packet *Evermore*. Five hours out of port, a terrible storm arose. Worse, behind the little sailing vessel, a monster of a whale suddenly appeared. Its jaws were opened wide, ready to swallow the ship and all aboard.

Desperately the crew emptied the hold of its cargo of apples and threw them overboard. The monster slowed to gobble crate after crate but always resumed pursuit.

The terrified sailors took the most desperate of measures. They drew lots. The loser was thrown overboard and vanished into the whale's mouth. Two more lots were drawn. Two more sailors were swallowed.

Granny Dobson watched with keen interest. At length, she spoke up. If she were cast into the sea, she said, the whale's hunger might be satisfied.

The idea dismayed the sailors. She reminded them of home and mother. But they agreed. At her request, they strapped her to her beloved rocking chair, which she had brought aboard. Over the side she went.

As soon as the sea monster gulped down Granny Dobson and her rocking chair, it disappeared beneath the waves. The *Evermore* survived the storm and reached Boston.

Three days later a whale drifted ashore. The sailors

of the *Evermore* saw it and realized it was the same whale. They got axes and cut it open.

Inside the stomach they found Granny Dobson. She sat in her chair, rocking contentedly and selling apples to the three sailors at a nickel apiece.

A couple of good ol' boys, Vernon and Earl, got caught in a budding hurricane off the coast of South Carolina when their boat's aged, wood-burning engine ran out of fuel. The situation looked desperate till Vernon had an idea. "Catch dogfish," he hollered. Each dogfish Earl caught, he threw over to Vernon, who rubbed its belly till it barked. After an hour they collected all the barks from the fish and fed them into the firebox and lit it. Before long, the old engine was chugging them to shore once more.

While Hal was fishing in Tennessee, a small snake swam by with a tadpole in its mouth. Hal snatched the snake to get the tadpole for bait. He gave the snake a shot of root beer and let it go. Five minutes later, the snake stuck its head over the side of the boat with another tadpole in its mouth. You know what? That snake kept Hal in tadpoles until the root beer ran out.

It was just before the 1939 Vermont deer season opened. As was his habit, the armchair outdoorsman was sounding off about how to hunt.

His name was Colonel W. Stoddard Williams. Sore-eared members of the fish and game club to which he belonged held that the *W* stood for Windbag. No one

had ever seen the colonel in the woods during hunting season.

Frank Matthews, a member of the club, finally had enough of the colonel's verbal handouts.

"Colonel," Matthews said, "if you know so dag-nabbed much about how to catch deer, why don't you go hunting and prove it?"

"I'll do that," the colonel replied defiantly.

At the end of opening day, the colonel had what he considered proof. He drove up to the deer weighing-in station.

"Put this one on the scales," he commanded.

The warden looked stunned for a moment. Then he said, "Colonel, we don't weigh goats here."

The most common outdoor tall tales concern the "one that got away." So, for the sake of variety, here's a fish story about the one that didn't.

A man from landlocked Kentucky was vacationing one winter in Miami. A sudden shower drove him to seek shelter. Quite by chance he darted into the Rod and Hunt Club.

He walked around the lobby slowly, looking at the mounted fish hanging on the walls till he came to a ten-foot tarpon. He stopped and stared at the huge fish in silence for a full minute. Then he roared, "The man who caught that fish is a dang-blamed liar!"

Solution

Encyclopedia knew that the ray gun had nothing to do with making the baby birds open their beaks for food.

The big blond boy was Wilford's partner, the detective quickly realized.

The big boy asked how the children would know when Wilford fired the gun.

Wilford answered that he'd touch the nest as he pulled the trigger.

Encyclopedia knew that *touching the nest,* not the gun, caused the baby birds to seek food.

Wilford merely exploited what the birds did naturally.

Most baby birds, even those too young to open their eyes, seek food when a parent bird alights on the nest.

By touching (and secretly pressing gently upon) the rim of the nest, Wilford matched the weight of a parent bird alighting.

The unseeing baby birds were fooled. They thought a parent had returned to the nest and opened their beaks to be fed.

EDUCATION

ADY 1182

DATE DU